Christopher Columbus

and the DISCOVERY of AMERICA

Christopher Columbus
1492

Christopher Columbus was an expert cartographer and navigator of Genoese origin.

Some say he could have been born in Portugal, Catalonia, Mallorca, Galicia...

- **Cartography:** It is the science that deals with the study and elaboration of maps.
- **Genoa:** City of Italy.

At the time of Christopher Columbus, people believed that the Earth was flat.

However, he argued that it was round and he intended to prove it.

N
W
E
S

To prove his theory, Christopher Columbus intended to reach the Indies by circumnavigating the world, crossing the Atlantic Ocean.

This would provide a new route to transport silk and spices, which are highly valued and expensive in Europe.

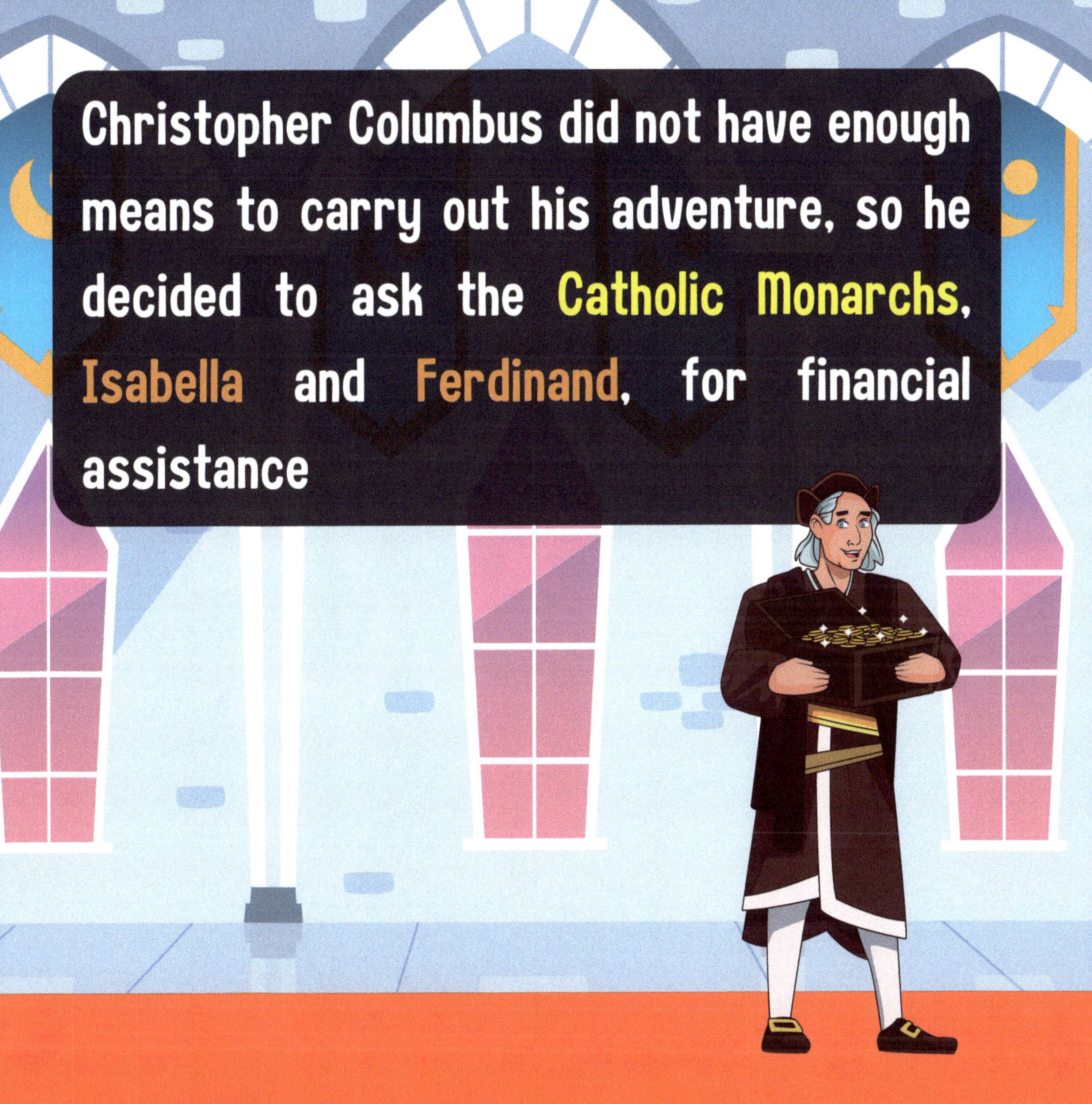

Christopher Columbus did not have enough means to carry out his adventure, so he decided to ask the Catholic Monarchs, Isabella and Ferdinand, for financial assistance

Thus, on August 3, 1492, our intrepid navigator set sail from the **port of Palos**.

- **Puerto de Palos:** River port of Palos de la Frontera (currently in Huelva, Spain).

For that first expedition, he had three ships and a crew of 120 men.

The names of the three ships used by Christopher Columbus on his first voyage were the Pinta, the Niña, and the Santa María.

The Santa Maria was a Nao, and the other two vessels were caravels.

- **Nao:** A large boat, equipped with a deck and sails, but no oars. It was mainly used between the 14th and 17th centuries.
- **Caravels:** Light sailing ships, used by Spain and Portugal in oceanic voyages in the 15th and 16th centuries.

Christopher Columbus traveled aboard the largest vessel, the Santa Maria

Before crossing the Atlantic, the expedition made a stop in the Canary Islands to repair the Pinta.

After more than a month at sea, the crew became furious due to the lack of food and water and the uncertainty of finding land.

The sailors **mutinied**, demanding their return to Spain.

- **Mutiny:** Group of people rebelling (refusing to obey) against authority.

Christopher Columbus asked for patience, as he was sure they would soon reach the mainland.

Shortly afterwards they could see some seagulls. This was a sign that they were approaching a coastal area

According to Columbus' ship's log, in the early morning of October 12, 1492, Rodrigo de Triana sighted land from the Pinta's mainmast, shouting...

- **Log:** Notebook in which Columbus wrote down the important events that occurred during navigation.
- **Mainmast:** The tallest mast or pole located in the center of the ship. It was where the basket was installed, from where the horizon was observed.

Land in sight!

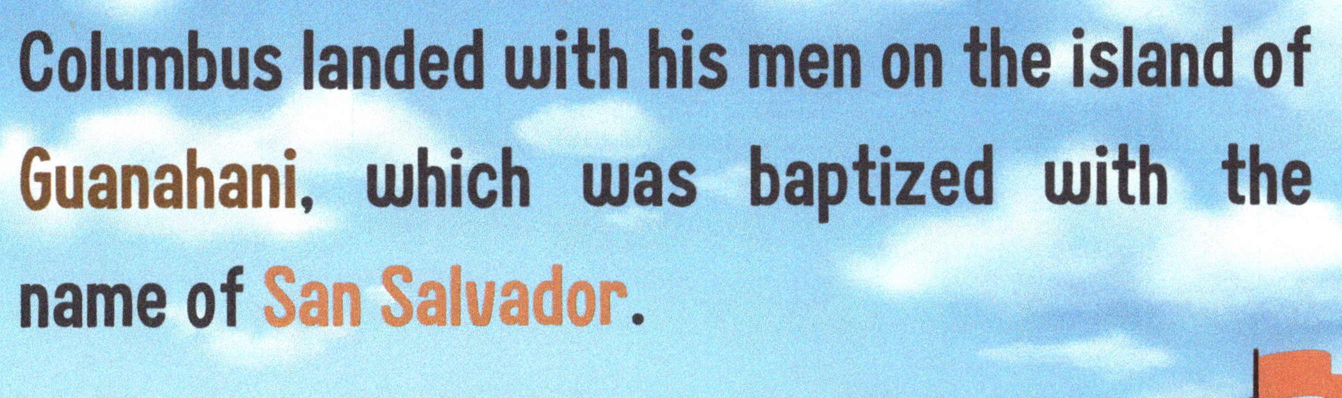

Columbus landed with his men on the island of Guanahani, which was baptized with the name of San Salvador.

When the new lands were discovered, an exchange of products and animals began.

Food products that were unknown in Europe, such as tomatoes, pineapple, cocoa, potatoes, corn, etc., were brought to Spain

Animals (horses, cows, sheep...) and plants (wheat, vines, olives...) arrived in America from Europe.

The Catholic Monarchs financed three new voyages, interested in the new trade route and the gold that Columbus brought from America.

On May 20, 1506, Christopher Columbus died, still believing he had discovered a new route to the East Indies.

Did you know that **Colombia** is named after Christopher Columbus?

However, he never set foot on Colombian soil.

It was Amerigo Vespucio (or Amerigo Vespucci) who realized that this route did not lead to the East Indies but to a new continent.

In his honor, the new continent was called America.

We have reached the end of our adventure!

I hope you enjoyed it and learned new things!

I want to ask you a favor so that this book reaches more people, and that is that you rate it with a sincere opinion on the platform where you purchased it.

With that small gesture, you will be helping me to carry on with new projects.

I can't wait to start creating my next book for you!

See you soon!

KEEP LEARNING...

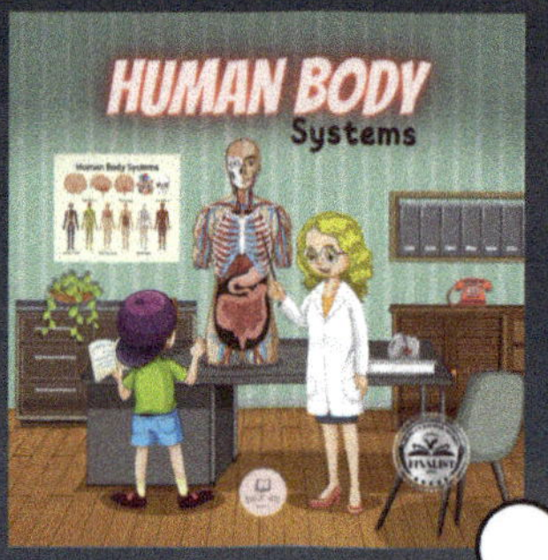

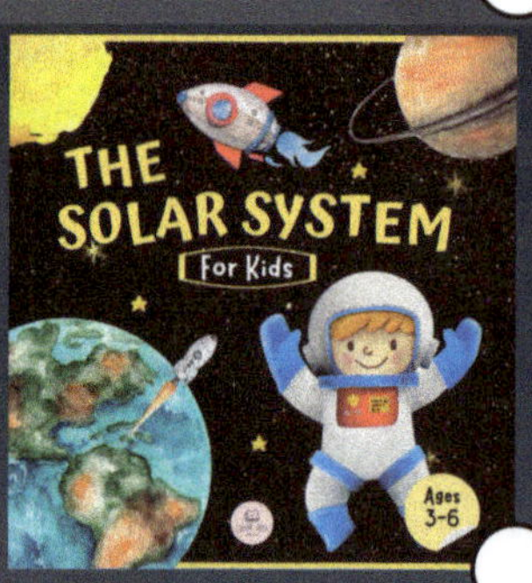

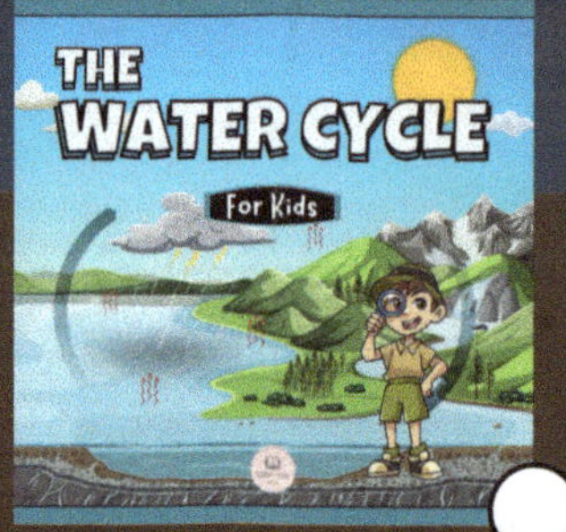

https://www.pge.me/childrensbooks

I HAVE A GIFT FOR YOU!

This Free eBook is for You!

SCAN ME

https://www.bit.ly/samueljohngift

I HOPE YOU LIKE IT!

The Steadfast Tin Soldier
SCAN ME
www.azonlinks.com/841269984X
SAMMIE EXPLORES THE SOLAR SYSTEM
Ages 3-6
SCAN ME
www.azonlinks.com/8412699866